Come With Me

A new and refreshing introduction
to the joys of meditation

by

MANNY PATEL Ph.D., D.O.

LIFE FOUNDATION PUBLICATIONS

By the same author

To Be Simply Human
Gift To The World

© Dr. Manny Patel 1990, 1991

First published in the United Kingdom in 1991 by
LIFE Foundation Publications
Maristowe House
Dover Street
Bilston
West Midlands WV14 6AL

ISBN 1 873606 00 1

Set in 12/14.5 New Century Schoolbook

Typeset by LHM Creative Consultants
Printed by Gibbons Barford Print, Willenhall, West Midlands

CONTENTS

CONTENTS continued...

CONTENTS continued...

About the author...

Dr. Manny Patel is one of the most inspired and dynamic teachers of meditation and yoga in the West at the present time. Born in Kenya, his early years were spent living close to nature and learning her secrets. During this time, he immersed himself in the ancient teachings. He arrived in England at the age of 12 leaving behind the simple lifestyle of his early years to embrace the complexities of western life.

Having been steeped in all aspects of life both in East and West – educational, cultural and spiritual – he has been able to bring together the two cultures and pass on the ancient wisdom of the East in a way which is meaningful and exciting to us in the West.

His fresh and vibrant approach to meditation has made him an outstanding leader in this field. He has an openness to all life and all traditions are honoured. His message has an appeal and relevance to all who are seeking relief from the stresses of modern life and searching for true inner contentment.

This is what Manny has been teaching in his unique and gentle way for the past 15 years. During this time his teachings have reached thousands of people across the world, bringing hope and inspiration to all who hear them.

How better can we sum up Manny's aims and vision than in his own words:

> **"In the simple language of the heart
> we meet each other."**

Why Meditate?

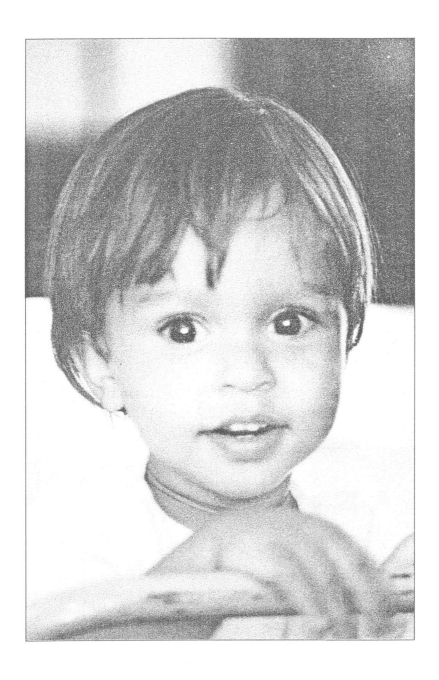

Modern medical research has confirmed that meditation has a profound influence on the harmful effects of stress. Many ancient traditions have been aware of this for centuries. The deep state of relaxation it promotes, reduces anxiety and tension, bringing about an improvement in general health and well-being. Meditation has been used successfully in the treatment of a whole spectrum of stress-induced diseases. These range from headaches and high blood pressure to arthritis and heart problems. It is also widely used in the management of life-threatening diseases such as cancer.

As we sit in silent meditation, an inner contentment arises naturally. This contentment banishes the agitations taking away our peace of mind. In the calmness which ensues we can see and accept ourselves as we truly are.

What Is Vipassana Meditation?

Vipassana means to observe things as they really are. It involves observation of ourselves – of our body and our mind. We see the totality of our relationship with ourselves, with other beings and with the world around us. We note our reactions to all this but do not get involved. We learn to leave behind our normal state of reactive 'doing' and enter into a state of simply 'being'.

"Meditation is a tool:

A way to explore the reality of life."

How To Use This Book

Before embarking upon the practice of meditation it is worth noting a few important principles.

The fruits of meditation can never be achieved by simply reading about it. Meditation has to be practised with an open heart and an open mind so that it becomes a living experience. "Practice brings perfection".

Each section in this book is intended to form a complete meditation for you to practise and enjoy. If you allow about 20 minutes for each section this will form a good basis for your daily practice. The most basic principles are introduced in the early chapters so, starting with chapter 1, read and familiarise yourself with the techniques. Re-read the chapter with a view to putting it into practice and then actually practise the meditation. Once you have mastered one section, move on to the next.

This is a progressive course. You will need to be thoroughly familiar with the principles you learn early on (for example, methods of body awareness) to put them into practice in the later sessions. You should also familiarise yourself with the names and locations of the seven major energy centres of the body (see page xxxi) as they will be referred to in some of the meditations.

By establishing your practice according to the principles outlined in the following pages and following the techniques given in this book, you will find that your life gains a whole new dimension. Remember, though, that to go deeply into the art of meditation, you need the guidance of a competent teacher. If you would like to take your meditation further or if you need any advice on the practice you are now beginning, qualified tutors are available at the L.I.F.E. Foundation centres in Bilston (West Midlands) and Bangor (North Wales). Regular sessions of Vipassana meditation are also held at both centres for you to attend.

The Correct Posture

The art of sitting

It is important to master the art of sitting correctly if you are to gain full benefit from your meditation practice. Traditionally you sit on the floor in the lotus posture. However, a cross-legged posture is perfectly acceptable. If this proves to be too difficult you can kneel on the floor or an upright chair or stool may be used. Hands should be resting gently on the lap.

You may find it easier to adopt the correct posture if you sit on the edge of a cushion as this will help tilt the lower back forward slightly. If necessary you can also support the knees with a cushion. In a kneeling posture a cushion between the thigh and calf may help the posture. If you are in a chair it is important to support yourself rather than leaning against the chair back.

Alignment of the spine

Once you have adopted the sitting position which is most comfortable for you, start to adjust your posture by gently straightening the spine. Becoming aware of the very base of the spine in contact with the floor, make sure that your weight is evenly balanced on either side and the lumbar region is pushed forwards.

Moving your awareness up towards the chest, push the vertebrae opposite the sternum forward and the vertebrae at the base of the neck backwards. This will lower the chin slightly. As you relax into this posture, imagine that there is a thread attached to the crown of your head which someone is pulling up, gently raising you towards the ceiling.

In this beautiful, natural posture check that your shoulders are free and all your limbs are relaxed. Ease out any tension which may remain in the facial muscles. Gently close your eyes and prepare to sit in stillness.

Correct Kneeling Posture

Correct Seated Posture

Establishing Your Practice

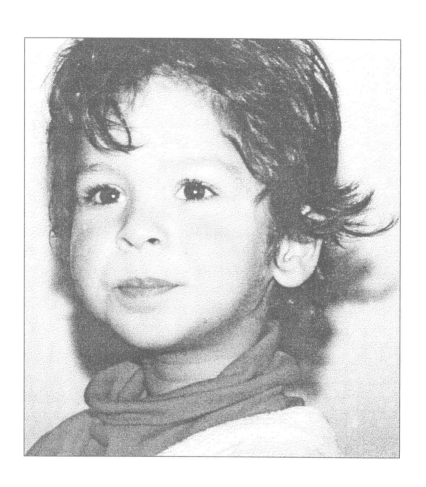

Make an appointment with yourself

You will find that the benefits of meditation are more apparent if you make it a regular habit, preferably setting aside the same times each day for your practice. It is recommended that you practise your meditation twice daily. Early morning when you arise and in the evening before going to bed are ideal times. If you cannot have a shower before meditating, try to awaken your body by washing hands and face with cold water.

Initially, you may find it difficult to sit still for any length of time. Don't worry if this is the case. Be full of confidence. Simply start by sitting for 5 minutes, making sure you don't cause any strain to your joints, and gradually build up the time until you can sit for 20 minutes without moving.

Try not to have a heavy meal just before meditating. If you must eat first, have a light snack or wait a while after a larger meal. You may find it helpful to set aside a set of loose, comfortable clothing which you keep just for meditation practice. A natural fibre such as cotton is preferable. You may also like to wrap a shawl or a light blanket round you each time you meditate.

It is beneficial if you can use the same place to meditate each time – if possible, in a warm well-ventilated room in which you can be relatively free from distractions. Make an appointment with yourself. Unplug the telephone, resolve that you will not react to the doorbell ringing or the sounds of life around you and make a commitment to yourself that you will devote the period alloted to meditation entirely to yourself.

As you begin to feel the benefits to your health and well-being, you will come to look forward to your daily appointments with yourself.

May you find true contentment as you embark upon this journey of discovery – the discovery of peace and stillness through which you will unfold your own inner perfection.

**"May we share this journey together
and bring laughter, joy
and true peace to everyone."**

Manny.

The Chakras

We know from ancient wisdom and modern physics that all matter is energy. A human being is powered by vital energy which enters through the crown of the head and is channelled downwards through seven main energy centres or chakras. These centres correspond to major nerve plexuses in the spinal column and are closely related to the principle endocrine glands of the body.

The profound effect of these chakras permeates our whole being. Not only does our physiological well-being reflect the efficiency of these energy powerhouses, but our emotional and mental behaviour patterns are also determined by them. Our skills and talents, our personal characteristics and degree of spiritual awareness are all an expression of this subtle energy system.

In short, we are the product of our chakras and for us to be completely healthy and balanced each chakra must be in a state of alignment so that energy can flow through it unimpeded. Any imbalances instigate 'dis-ease' on all levels of our existence.

The meditational practices outlined in this book will, if practised regularly and with attentiveness, help you to maintain a state of perfect balance. As harmony arises within you, positive, ennobling qualities emerge, transmuting the self-dimension into a joyous and highly esteemed life.

In each chakra we have the past, the present and the future. The future is nothing more than the past altered in the present. The key to this wisdom is contained within the exploration of the vital chakras of the human body.

Sahasrara
Crown
"contentment"

Ajna
Brow
"intuition"

Vishuddha
Throat
"self-expression"

Anahata
Heart
"compassion"

Manipura
Solar
"will"

Swadhisthana
Sacral
"desire"

Mooladhara
Base
"regeneration"

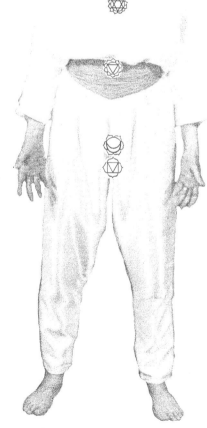

Come
With
Me

Unfoldment...

It is important to realise how effortless the process of meditation should be.

It's like surfing.

Imagine you are riding effortlessly on the crest of a wave which carries you all the way to the shore.

Meditation is like that.

Too often we try too hard to make things happen; and the harder you try the less things happen.

Just let it unfold.

You will find that the more peaceful you are with yourself the greater will be the healing.

Touch The Inner Harmony

*Meditation
is
effortless*

*Just let it
unfold*

Increasing your compassion...

Remember that the people you love are also meant to be helped by your progress.

You are not on a selfish pursuit.

It is meant to be

an act of **transformation**

an act of increasing your **compassion**

so that creation itself benefits from your presence and your works.

Listening...

From the **stillness** of your own being learn to **listen**...
      to the sounds of nature outside ...
      to your own presence...

Listening is a means of inner revelation.

Relaxing...

As you sit, bring your presence to your body...
as it sits
very **calm**, very **still**, very **content**.

On every exhalation, **relax** your body:
legs and feet
arms and hands
the shoulders.

Let the **eyes** and **face** become softer, more peaceful.
And go yet more deeply into that **softness** and **peace**.

The inner harmony...

Try and see the **inner vision**, the **inner creativity**, with your eyes closed.

> Let your mind be at peace.

On every exhalation, let the body relax, the eyes become softer and more peaceful.

> **SMILE**.

Let the smile **create a stillness and peace within your being**.

Make a gentle **conviction** within your heart that you will do everything you can with

> your body, mind and spirit

> in order to touch the **inner harmony**.

Accepting...

In the **stillness** that will unfold before you, many new revelations will come to you and **transformations** will take place.

Don't judge these transformations.

Accept them because it is the very nature of your being that is being explored and exposed.

Allow yourself to flow.

Letting go...

If you want to grow, you have to let go.

If you let go a little bit, you will grow a little bit;

let go a bit more and you will grow even more;

if you **let go completely**, then **total growth** takes place.

A beautiful realisation.

Be happy with yourself...

Y*ou are gently beginning to move. It's only a matter of letting go and it's important to let go of your conditioning as much as you can.*

A*s human beings we are conditioned to flow out to other people. There is a time for flowing out but, at other times when you are trying to gather and conserve, it's important to be* **enclosed in your own self.**

W*e have always been taught to interact with people. Very rarely do we just sit quietly with people and still feel comfortable. But we should be happy with as few words, as few gestures and as few interactions as possible.*

Focus *on this simplicity.*

Accept Life

For What It Is

*Make a commitment to yourself
that you will see things
as they are...*

*without any bias
or
pre-conceived ideas.*

Be open to life...

Come to appreciate the **silence** of your own being.

See the glory in the **stillness** of your mind.

Allow the tension to fade away from your body.

Let us welcome the day
with an **open heart**,
welcoming Mother Nature.

Gently with your eyes closed,

arms open,

palms facing upwards,

raise your hands to welcome the Sun.

Feel the **warmth** and **energy**
as you embrace the sun.

Let the **healing grace**
flow out from your hands.

Then gently let your hands come to rest on your knees
with the palms still facing upwards and

feel totally **open to all life**.

Relax...

your partially opened eyes

so they are not focussing on anything
in particular

your body

so it melts into nothingness

And be aware of the breathing process.

Breathing...

up to the top
of your head

down to the floor
of your pelvis

rhythmically, calmly, peacefully.

Accept life...

Try not to have any expectations or pre-judgements.
Let things be just as they are.

Ask yourself:

"Am I willing to accept things just as they are?"

"Am I willing to accept life for what it is?"

**"Without any expectation
or pre-judgement?"**

When the answer becomes 'YES' close your eyes.

Breath awareness...

Once acceptance has taken place, follow the out-breath and come into a state of breath awareness:

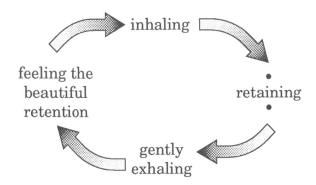

inhaling

feeling the
beautiful
retention

retaining

gently
exhaling

Now gently and slowly count your exhalations up to ten, letting the mind be focussed and relaxed.

Then for the next 30 seconds open the eyes just a fraction and sit in absolute stillness. Even the breath should be imperceptible.

Let it just happen naturally...

Then relax becoming aware of your contact with the floor and your presence in the room as you close your eyes.

The light of conviction...

Bring your hands together in your lap.

Come to appreciate your conviction that you will see things **as they are** without any pre-conceived ideas.

And in the centre of your palms, with your palms close together, imagine a gentle light —

the **light of conviction**.

Gently take your palms towards your heart centre and absorb that golden light into your chest – as a little promise to yourself to see things as they are.

Let the light gently expand until it fills your **whole being**.

Conviction – the foundation of all liberation.

Be still...

*W*e don't have to do a great deal to be happy with ourselves.

*T*here is a very beautiful quote in the Bible:

"Be still and know that I am God"

*I*t is telling us something very special: to discover God and to be one with all that you are, you have to be still — not just physically but mentally, emotionally and spiritually as well.

*T*his is the purpose of meditation, stillness and prayer. Stillness evokes within us a sense of immortality and that is what you will captivate — the stillness to know God yourself.

Captivate
The
Moving Energy

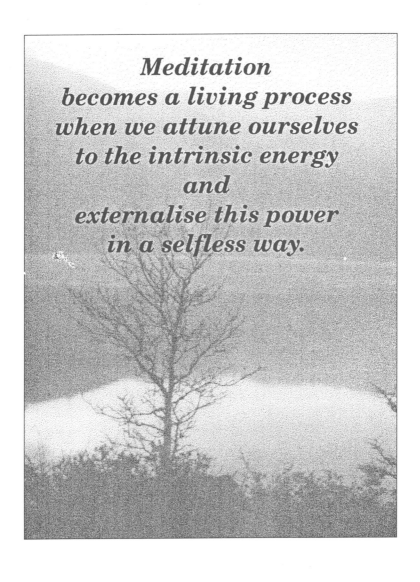

Meditation
becomes a living process
when we attune ourselves
to the intrinsic energy
and
externalise this power
in a selfless way.

Welcome the day...

As you welcome the morning sun, try to appreciate the coming of a new day, a new beginning of the freshness that is living, moving and inspiring.

As a gentle preparation to the day

pay homage

to the Great Spirit

to your parents

to your teachers

to the Inspiring Ones who
have yet to come into
your own life.

Be aware of your breathing...

and with each breath appreciate

the new living force that enters
and rejuvenates

the depth and gentleness
of the breath

the retention deep within the
centre of your own being.

Be aware.

Be in the Now-ness...

And **be aware** of your body as you take the breath of love into

> your feet and legs
>
> your arms and hands
>
> your abdomen and chest
>
> the senses in the region of
> your head – the highest
> point of your being.

As you become aware of them, **relax** them and **bless** them for their presence.

As every cell in your body breathes in and out, relax every part.

Wherever the attention wanders to, relax that part. Be aware but very **still**.

Just watch and observe everything that happens in the few minutes as stillness captivates you. Allow the captivation to be **total**.

Feel, appreciate and welcome the stillness.

Feel the peace...

Learn to appreciate the feeling of peace that pervades you.

If you can just catch a glimpse of the divinity that you are, your function will have been achieved.

Once you've touched that very gently, just for a split second, you will undergo a very rapid and total transformation. In that transformation you will find a new joy which you cannot describe in words.

Be One

With The Earth

Where there is stillness
there we shall find peace.

Where there is hope
there we shall find humanity.

Awakening to a new day...

From a point of stillness greet the morning sun
and the awakening day.

Greet the first breath you take.

Listen to the sounds of life around you.
Let your being emanate the radiant sun.

Relax and bring peace to

> your compassionate hands
> your arms, your legs.

Be **aware** of

> the presence of the life force
> within your body

> the contact of your body
> with Mother Earth.

Be **grateful** to Mother Earth

> for her support and

> for **giving you a place
> in the universe**.

A unique place.

Acknowledge the connection between you and Mother Earth...

Gently place your hands on the floor in front of you. Let rays of rainbow light flow from your fingertips and merge with the very centre of the planet Earth.

Once you feel yourself in touch with the core of the planet, honour that beautiful connection. Concentrate on it and keep your vision on it. Do not let the light and connection be broken. Let your whole being shine.

Return your hands to your knees.

Become aware of

the **intensification of the light** between you and the centre of the earth. Let the cord that joins the two of you grow and strengthen.

your **breathing**. Be aware of the expansion and contraction of the abdomen and let that be the pulsation between you and Mother Earth.

the **lightness** in your body.

The cleansing process has started.

Remember Mother Earth...

for her support and contact, and
for the bond between you.

In reality she is your mother
sustaining and nourishing and nurturing you.

Always

Always

The essence of peacefulness...

After a short time of total profound silence you will find something happens – a small capturing of the essence. And in that essence the spirit shines.

Try to remember that peacefulness is never achieved unless you practise being at one with yourself. So be as sincere and positive as you can.

At each stage as we go along just observe yourself. See what is happening and try to understand the way the mind and spirit are connected. Once you do understand it, you will not be a slave to circumstances. You will actually be able to work by yourself in whatever environment you find yourself.

Awaken
The
Spirit Within

In the peace of early morning

we discover

the

silent guide

within us.

Be still...

Be **still** in your mind and body, **relaxing** each part of your body in turn, moving from —

the feet to

the hands to

the face.

Let your forehead and eyes be relaxed and in the space within your inner vision just see the word

Relaxation

come into being.

Let that word assist you in calming your mind and the entirety of your body.

Breathing is life...

Begin to **observe** and put your **whole attention** into...

The expansion and contraction of the abdomen

The air leaving your nostrils

The rising of the chest on inhalation

Holding the breath

The silent exhalation as the chest and abdomen contract

The relaxation that sets behind your eyelids as you are consciously aware of the breathing.

Slowly and softly... relax

With every **exhalation**

become more **peaceful** and **relaxed**

Allow the **breathing** to happen **naturally**

becoming the **awareness** behind the breathing

listening to the sounds and echoes around you

being aware of **life** around you

noticing the **silent energies** within your body.

You **are** the **silent presence**.

Awaken your body...

Breathe more consciously and deeply now
becoming aware of

>the skin which encapsulates your body

>your arms and legs

>the straightness and alertness of your back

>each sound which activates something
>in your being.

Gently relaxing your body even more
slowly take your hands to your face.
Feel each part of it slowly and silently.

**There is nowhere to go,
nothing to rush into.**

Just appreciate the presence of all the features as you
allow your body to awaken.

Beautiful, silent presence.

In stillness we find home...

*W*hen there is stillness in the mind, one finds that compassion grows. And in the growth of compassion there is an emanation of love for your family and friends. Inspiration comes. From that love and inspiration, success is born. From the growth of success in life, there is peace in the nation and there is peace in the world.

*I*t is, therefore, our duty as human beings to achieve and recognise a state of peacefulness so that the whole of creation is at peace.

*L*et your vision expand in these thoughts of consciousness...

*L*et your motive encompass the whole of God's creation...

*A*nd let these tears of stillness bring about a sense of acceptance of yourself as you are now.

Let
Compassion
Arise

Compassion
plays a very important part
in purification.

When you let it grow
you will find
a great many burdens leave
you.

Compassion,
Oh compassion
I welcome you.

Let go...

As you move on gently, have a beautiful thought in your heart:

a thought of **letting go**.

Let go of everything that has ever happened to you; let go of all the despondency, aggression and injustice that have taken place in your life.

The way to do it is to be present in the now-ness.

This is the way of **compassion**.

Be aware...

of your **body**

scan your body quickly, relaxing each part in turn

create a lightness in your head

feel the beautiful warmth that glows in your heart

rub your eyes gently until they become very relaxed and soft

Be aware...

of your **breath**

take deep inhalations down to the base of your spine, hold the breath for a while, then gently exhale

count your out-breaths up to 10.
Focus your whole attention on the counting and if your mind wanders start from 1 again.

become aware of the inhalation and exhalation not forcing it but just watching it happen.

watching your breath with your attention on the abdomen, just **sit in that awareness** for five minutes **in total stillness.**

Open your heart...

Gently and slowly **half open your eyes** then close them again. Do this a few times until the energy comes to the focus of the eyes so that compassion rises and opens the higher centres.

Focus on the palms of your hands and feel the lightness and warmth of the energy you carry there.

Gently **prolong the exhalation**, focus on it and be aware of any sensations that arise.

Moving on, as you focus once again on the out-breath, **let your body become lighter** by itself. Just let it go and it will happen. Open your heart and let compassion arise.

Slowly take your hands to your face and rub it gently; partially open your eyes, look at the floor for a few seconds; and gently open your compassionate eyes.

Discovery of expansion...

You discover that when you are dealing with subtle energy, you need to give it space. It needs room to expand.

We used to have a camel which we kept tied to a post in the garden. It was always trying to get away and used to pull the post out of the ground, however firmly we had secured it. And yet, if we let it loose, it never wandered far from the house.

If we reflect on this, we realise that the mind is very similar. Poke it and it will create a lot of disturbance; but if you can just let it be and focus your energy on something else, it calms down and becomes a very peaceful servant.

And, of course, when the mind is calm, all sorts of beautiful things emerge —

compassion, kindness, love.

Capture The Essence

When the mind is calm

compassion

kindness

and

love

emerge.

Unite with Mother Earth...

Embracing the sound of silence, begin the journey by acknowledging our relationship with Mother Earth.

Gently lower your hands to the floor, asking for the blessings and guidance of the force of Mother Earth.

Then, taking your hands back onto your knees – palms facing upwards – receive the blessings from the higher planes.

We are all recipients of the forces around us.

Body awareness...

Mentally massage your whole body from the feet
upwards

    relaxing each part

    then feeling the heart become warm
as the ribcage expands and contracts.

Now
let us begin
to
tame the mind

Breath awareness...

Your breath is
peaceful, **slow** and **controlled**...

Move effortlessly into the cycle of
    inhaling, retaining
    exhaling, holding.

Let the exhalations become longer and more peaceful.

Focus all your attention on your breath, keeping the mind gently occupied.

If the mind does wander too much, gently re-open your eyes for a few seconds, then close them again.

Choiceless awareness...

Keeping the body absolutely still
stop counting and just focus on the

awareness.

Let all noises just drift by
let all events take place around you.

Try to be in the pure **awareness** of **observation**

choiceless awareness...

Sounds come and go but you are still there...
Notice the beautiful silence...

Then gently relax your body...
become aware of your eyes,
rub them gently with your hands and open them.

The inner stillness...

*B*ehind your closed eyes there is a fascinating
new world:

> the Kingdom of Heaven that
> the Lord Christ described;
>
> the Kingdom of peace and equanimity
> that Buddha talked about;
>
> a place of stillness, an inner sanctuary
> that Krishna described in his youth.

*A*nd for yourself, there awaits the greatest discovery: it is from that inner source of stillness that
all things come into being.

We are here so that the Self meets the Self.

The Self
Meets
The Self

From

the inner source

of stillness

let all things

come into being.

Awareness...

Let your whole **body** be **still** and **relaxed**.

Allow your breathing to unfold your back, opening each and every vertebra from the neck to the base.

Appreciate the **compassion** and **charity** which pour out through your **hands**

and

the **potent awareness** in your **head**,
the **light** at the very centre of the skull.

Create a Golden Light...

Establish a beautiful golden light at the centre of your being in the forehead – like the glowing sun.

Let it glow and expand on every exhalation until it totally envelops you.

Gently count the exhalations up to ten and let the light emanate beyond the boundary of your physical self throughout the room.

Feel the warmth of the golden light all around you.

Purify yourself...

Focus at the base of the spine and concentrate the golden light there.

As you breathe in raise the light along the spine,
    purifying your being.

Partially open your eyes for a few seconds, keeping them soft and focussed into infinity. Accept what you see for what it is without judgement.

Then close your eyes again,
    resting and purifying.

Focus on the pure nature of the breath.

The breath of life...

Maintain **awareness** on

the air leaving and entering your nose.

For five minutes, in absolute silence and without any movement of your body or deviation of your mind, watch the nature of your breathing.

If any sensation arises at body level,

watch it rising

put your attention on it for a while,

let it dissolve

then come back to your breathing

and

be silent with **peaceful watchfulness**.

As the **healing force** circulates round your body, let it heal and revitalise you and bring lightness to your being.

Feel your presence in the all-pervading **oneness** that you are.

Let the Self meet the Self.

Be at peace...

As the purification and expansion of your being take place, you will find that many things come to the surface: pains, sensations that you may not have felt for a long time, emotions and experiences.

It's like a form of purification, removing the blocks and inhibitions and allowing your mind to be at rest as inclinations and tendencies emerge and dissipate from the depth of your consciousness and subconsciousness.

All sorts of memories will emerge – perhaps happy, maybe traumatic. Don't try to suppress them but see them for what they are because with them will be precipitated a great deal of unwanted material, leaving behind a tremendous sense of freedom, recognition and long-lasting peace.

Life
Is

Harmony

*Let the peace
of the whole creation
surround your very being*

let peace be around you

let peace be above you

and

*let a deep peace reside within
you.*

Simply be...

Be open with your heart and spirit
as you become aware of:

the time of year

the time of day

your place in the universe

noises coming and going

the way your body resonates.

You have nothing special to do,
nowhere particular to go.

Just simply be.

Feel the breath of life...

Every breath is a new birth; it is a recognition that life renews itself from moment to moment. Make each breath special and feel how wonderful it is to be alive.

Be conscious of your breath.

Relax with your breath.

On the **in-breath**
welcome the sun and **life**
into your being.
Let the **inner radiance**
gently grow.

On the **out-breath**
extend the exhalation;
flow out with it and
try to reach the
other side of the room.

Gently start to breathe out
through the tips of your fingers
breathing out **compassion**.
Let compassion grow
with each expansion.

Let your heart open...

In the silence let your mighty heart open

> feel the presence of love reaching out
> all around you

> notice your hands growing and magnifying
> your compassionate nature

> feel your mind become very cool, very light
> and very fresh

> be aware of the feelings of lightness or warmth
> starting to emerge in different parts of the body.

Focus your entire mind on the silence for a few
moments.

Become aware of your fingers.

Gently massage your eyes with your fingertips,
inhaling deeply and awakening your body.

Open your eyes, really feeling one with yourself.

We are all one...

We all need to remind ourselves why we are
here and to recognise that each one of us is related
to every other being in the whole universe by what
could be called the 'divine light'. And that light
which connects us all, is to be acknowledged.

It is something that we should be able to feel to
such a degree that we realise that everyone we
share this planet with is part of our own being.
People who need help, people who have sorrow,
people who are less fortunate than us – on a
material, spiritual or emotional plane – all need
assistance and sharing.

Our purpose is to intensify our own mode of
conduct to be able to appreciate and bring out our
talents through the art of awakening the spiritual entity within us.

In this respect it is very important that we learn
to trust each other. Trust is vital in that it creates
an openness in the heart and mind – creating a
mind which is patient and tolerant and willing
to listen, to learn and to grow.

Key To Freedom

Just as every raindrop
which falls, has a place
which is right for it

so too

will every breath you take
find a perfect place
in your being.

Breath control...

Within the quietude of your own presence, come to relax as quickly as you can.

Become the **controller of your breath,**

Extend the inhalations,
then the exhalations
as you establish the pattern of

breathing in...   retaining...
breathing out...   retaining...

Breathing is the **key** to **freedom**.

Peace...

Breathe in and retain the breath
    affirming the words

Peace   *Peace*   *Peace*

Breathe out and retain the emptiness
    affirming

Peace   *Peace*   *Peace*

Do this five times.

Stilling the mind...

Bringing yourself into a natural state of
pure awareness...

Open your eyes gently and focus on the tip of your nose.

As you **inhale**
    take your head back
        bring your sternum forward
        ...still focussing on the tip of the nose.

Hold the breath and the position for a few seconds and

As you **exhale**
    close your eyes
        bring the head to face forward.

Repeat this until the mind becomes totally still.

Place the tip of your tongue on the roof of your mouth behind the upper front teeth. This is the Kechari mudra of peace.

Relax and remain totally still,
focussing your attention totally
both on the breathing and on the tip of the tongue.

If **sensations** come,
    watch them
        and they will **disappear**.

Use your breath as a guide.

Just as you become used to your own shadow, you become sensitised to your own breathing patterns, hence awakening your own life-giving force.

This is the secret to your own self-realisation and freedom.

Appreciate the feeling of being
totally at peace.

You are stillness...

Once again, as the morning begins, a new life beginning takes place, a new seed generates. For it is the same old sun that rises above the horizon and awakens the whole of nature. You are that very sun which gives life to all things in existence.

Allow other things to move around you; but from your own standpoint **you are very still**.

There's no need to react or get upset, no need to create sorrow or frustration. Notice how still you are.

Within your awareness the noises come; within your awareness the noises move away again; but you are still.

Learn to see all things from that point of stillness.

A Journey

Of

Purification

Like a child feeling earth
like a child appreciating
flowers in the garden

let us begin our journey.

Become free...

Beginning with a **fresh**, **open**, **accepting** and **non-judging** mind, scan the body and mind, easing out any pockets of tension.

As the body becomes light and peaceful, allow your vision to gently expand within your own mind's eye.

Free the creative you and let us begin the journey.

Allow the child in you to expand...

See yourself sitting and
gently rising into the sky
peacefully...
very silently...
higher and higher...
just like the clouds gently drifting upwards.

Above you in the distance you can see
a **golden light** emanating.

Allow the child in you to expand towards it

and take you underneath this light

— a golden waterfall —

What a joyous sight and experience.

Breathe in the golden light...

Allow the golden light from the waterfall to bathe and flow down your

head

    face

        chest

            abdomen

                legs

                    soles

refreshing and **cleansing**
each part it touches.

Raise the golden light...

On the **in-breath:**

Raise the same golden light
from the soles of the feet
to the mooladhara centre
at the base of the spine.

On the **out-breath:**

Pause at this centre,
feel the purification and
observe any sensations
that arise.

On each **in-breath,**   On each **out-breath,**
raise the golden light   &   pause at that centre,
to the next centre   feeling the purification.

In this way, raise the light through each centre in turn
until it reaches the highest centre on the crown of your
head.

Do this three times altogether

then

gently descend from the waterfall
coming back to an earthly plane.

Breath awareness...

Now notice your **breathing** at the **heart centre**.

Establish a conscious rhythm of breathing:

inhale,   retain
exhale,   retain

as you remain still
for a few moments longer.

Gently rub your face and slowly open your eyes.

When time disappears...

When we dwell within the spirit, we discover that time only has meaning as long as the mind is present. In the sphere of the spirit, time seems to disappear. In silence, time dissolves and four minutes seem like 20 seconds.

It is a very beautiful thing when time becomes timeless because you are allowing a concept which has always held you to be eradicated.

When we become timeless, we are nearer to the state of recognising what we truly are. In joy and ecstasy when we are laughing there is no time.

Gift Of Love

Learn to create an openness in your heart

*Know you are
a growing, expanding, caring
and loving individual.*

Uncovering the true 'I' ness...

Within the **stillness** you are gently uncovering **the**
true personality

— the true 'I'ness —

and this becomes the greatest religion of all times:

the religion of
what you are at this very present moment.

Relax...

Let your **eyes** relax and be aware of any colours, im-
ages or lights that come before them. Just let them be
present without judgement or reaction.

Focus on the breath...

Allow your body to
pulsate with breath.

Focus on the **coolness**
of the **in-breath** at
the base of the nose.
Become very attentive.
If you miss it on the
first breath, try it
again and again until
the prana becomes
a living force.

Now focus on the **warmth**
of the **out-breath**.
It is the out-breath
which is very **relaxing**
and holds the key to
stability.

For a few moments open your
mouth very slightly and
breathe through the mouth.
Feel the **light** that enters
the mind's eye ...
then close your mouth
when you feel ready.

Now **focus** on the
emptiness at the end of
the out-breath and before
the in-breath.
Capture it and sit in it
for a few seconds.
Pure awareness resides
there - in the emptiness
of breath.

Become an observer...

Prepare your body for **stillness**. Allow it to relax into a state of **total attunement**. Let it go and become an **observer**, waiting for the gap after each silent out-breath.

That void gives you an opportunity to be with the **pure subjectiveness** of yourself.

In this **awareness** watch any sensations that arise with an **equanimous** state of mind.

Be one with the whole of nature...

Sitting in this **purity**, allow your **awareness** to **follow** and allow your energy to touch the clouds in the sky.

Let it go beyond the valleys into the mountains and rivers. Breathe into the trees, through the woods, forests, rivers and oceans.

We are **unified** with all parts of nature.

This is true detachment.

The inner vision opens...

Let there be a gentle gaze in your eyes as you half open them, watching whatever is before you with a sense of peace.

Then close your eyes and focus on:

    your breathing...

        bare awareness...

            the ajna centre...

        You can almost feel a very gentle light descending within your being from far above as the inner vision opens. Whatever sensation you feel in the ajna centre, appreciate it. Let a beautiful awakening take place.

    Let the Spirit within you be free...
        Let it be free.

Be yourself...

It is said in our tradition that whereas a human being has to fight negativity or evil, a man of peace doesn't have to do anything but be himself.

All of us have many challenges in life – financial problems, human problems, emotional problems. These are all chains that are bound to us and which bring us sorrow. In order to free ourselves from the chain, we have to break the links; we have to relax and let go.

Be Free

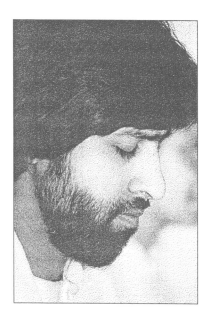

Suffering is self-perpetuating.

Remove the cause and the suffering will leave by itself.

An end to suffering...

The most important emotion which seems to affect us and interfere with our lives, is that of **suffering**.

Suffering is self-perpetuating because of the **greed**, **anger** and **illusion** which we carry with us.

When you are meditating and absorbed into your own self, it is important to realise that it is these attributes which are bringing suffering to your doorstep.

Greed: Over-eating is one manifestation of greed. No doubt one day it will bring some sort of suffering to you, affecting the way you think, the way you feel. Please think about this. You must realise the power of greed.

Anger: We do not always appreciate anger in its real sense. To be impatient and intolerant is also to be angry. These two are brothers and sisters of greed.

Illusion: Suffering that arises from illusion is something that is rarely understood by most of us. Subtle aspects of illusion come to us in the way of daydreaming – perhaps in a very negative and detrimental way.

It is, therefore, very important to **appreciate the way we live our daily lives** and see how quickly most things fall into these three categories.

Remember that because you carry these three things with you – in your heart, in your mind, in your body, in your speech, in your actions, in your feelings – the very guardian of suffering sits next to you.

Remove and **transform** these three things and **suffering** will leave by itself.

Keep your motives pure...

Remember that no matter how much you practise prayer and spirituality, you are not going to get a tremendous reward from it from an external source. You find that if you do seek rewards, the peace goes away very quickly.

So you just learn to introspect your peace. That means that your motive is guided not by the ego but by the Spirit.

Practise purity in your motives. Be independent from results. Seek no recognition but feel into the way the Spirit wishes to flow and go with it.

Always know that good people and those in need will be around you when your heart is pure. If it is full of burdens, selfishness or greed, it won't happen.

So look at your life again and say:

"What is it that I'm doing wrong?"
"What is it that I'm doing right?"
"How can I make that peace within me grow?"

And contemplate on these thoughts.

Keep an open heart...

You will begin to feel a **lightness**

> **in your being**
> **in your clarity of thought**
> **in your appreciation of simple things**.

You are trying to watch things as they are – not how you would like them to be – seeing things in their true colours; seeing things in their simplicity.

Try to keep an **open mind** and a very **open heart**.

With that openness something even more beautiful can happen, something even more divine. It will only take a split second.

Be prepared always.

The L.I.F.E. Foundation School of Therapeutics

The L.I.F.E. Foundation was established by Dr. Manny Patel in 1975 to promote the principles of wholeness and health. His work rapidly spread from the two main centres in Bangor (North Wales) and Bilston (West Midlands) throughout the country and into Europe, India and the U.S.A.

As founder director of the L.I.F.E. Foundation School of Therapeutics, Dr. Patel established a number of highly popular and successful courses. In addition to holding regular sessions of Vipassana Meditation, Dr. Patel and his senior tutors run courses in Therapeutic Dru Yoga, Stress Management, Healing, Creative Visualisation, Self-Esteem, Gaia and Global Ecology, Diet and Nutrition, Counselling and Psychotherapy.

Seminars and conferences are held throughout Great Britain, Europe, U.S.A. and India and Dr. Patel has successfully established a global network of holistically oriented groups and individuals. He works with cancer self-help groups, health groups, yoga societies and medical and educational institutions. There are close links between the L.I.F.E. Cancer Centre, also established by Dr. Patel, and the National Health Service. The L.I.F.E. Foundation and L.I.F.E. Cancer Centre are non-profit making organisations.